KIDS MAKE IT BETTER

IT BETTER

A WRITE-IN, DRAW-IN JOURNAL

Suzy Becker

WORKMAN PUBLISHING
NEW YORK

Library of Congress Cataloging-in-Publication Data is available.

ISBN 978-0-7611-5845-5

Workman books are available at special discounts when purchased in bulk for premiums and sales promotions as well as for fund-raising or educational use. Special editions of book excerpts can also be created to specification. For details, contact the Special Sales Director at the address below or send an e-mail to specialsales@workman.com.

Design by Raquel Jaramillo and Netta Rabin

Workman Publishing Company, Inc.
225 Varick Street
New York, NY 10014-4381
www.workman.com

Printed in the U.S.A.
First printing April 2010

10 9 8 7 6 5 4 3 2 1

For Aurora, Henry and Hildy

with thanks to Savannah, Raquel, Netta, Robby, Edite,
Rosie, Liz and Lorene

In most loving memory of Ted Sizer

Welcome to This Book!

When I was 7, I learned that a 10¢ packet of salt and sugar (oral rehydration therapy) could save another 7-year-old's life. I thought, "10¢? I can save someone's life for 10¢?!"

me   my friend

That summer, my friend and I set up a lemonade stand. We sold 850 cups of lemonade and we sent UNICEF the $85 we earned. By our calculations, we'd saved 850 lives. That's a powerful feeling.

You can save people's or animals' or plants' lives, too. I made this book to help you get started. There are 24 problems for you to solve (plus extra pages in the back so you can record and solve more on your own). All you need is some time and your imagination (and a pencil with an eraser, some crayons, paints, maybe some snacks).

When you are ready to put your imagination into action, turn to the Action Plan—the green pages at the end of the book. Your plan may not actually solve the problem (my lemonade stand didn't), but you will have made the world a better place. And if you keep giving the world's problems your time and your imagination, you may, one day, make one of them go away.

—Suzy Becker

P.S. Save this book so I can say I told you so.

PROBLEM

Air pollution makes it hard for plants, animals, and people to breathe, and it causes global warming. How can we clean up our air?

SOLUTION
(by Johanna, age 8)

"I would have all the people get a hose and wash the pollution away every day. It might make a rainbow."

YOUR SOLUTION

How would you clean up our air?

_____

_____

_____

_____

_____

_____

_____

A PICTURE OF YOUR SOLUTION

PROBLEM

There is not enough clean water for all the living things on our planet. How can we fix that?

SOLUTION
(by Jackie, age 9)

"Have scientists make fish that love to eat tons of pollution."

THIS REALLY WORKS!

A silver carp can eat twice its body weight (up to 60 pounds) of blue-green algae. So China used tens of millions of silver and grass carp to clean up Taihu Lake, its third-largest freshwater lake and the source of drinking water for 17 million people.

YOUR SOLUTION

What do you think we can do to take better care of our water?

_____

_____

_____

_____

_____

_____

_____

YES, KIDS CAN!

Ryan Hreljac, age 7

Ryan's first-grade teacher told his class that many African children did not have clean water to drink. Ryan started doing chores to raise enough money to buy one water well, and then he never stopped! Ryan has now raised enough money to provide water wells for half a million Africans.

PROBLEM

Sometimes people disagree with each other. Disagreements can lead to fighting or even to war. How would you make people stop fighting and just get along?

SOLUTION

(by Adrienne, age 9)

"The whole country should have a big protest together, and all the children should hold up signs that make people stop and laugh and think about what they're doing."

What would you do to help people stop fighting and get along?

A PICTURE OF YOUR SOLUTION

PROBLEM

How would you fix someone's broken heart?

SOLUTION

(by Tiffany, age 8)

"Give them some hug bubbles and
love them very much."

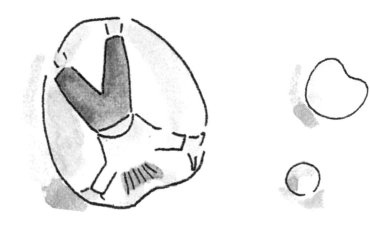

How would you fix a broken heart?

A PICTURE OF YOUR SOLUTION

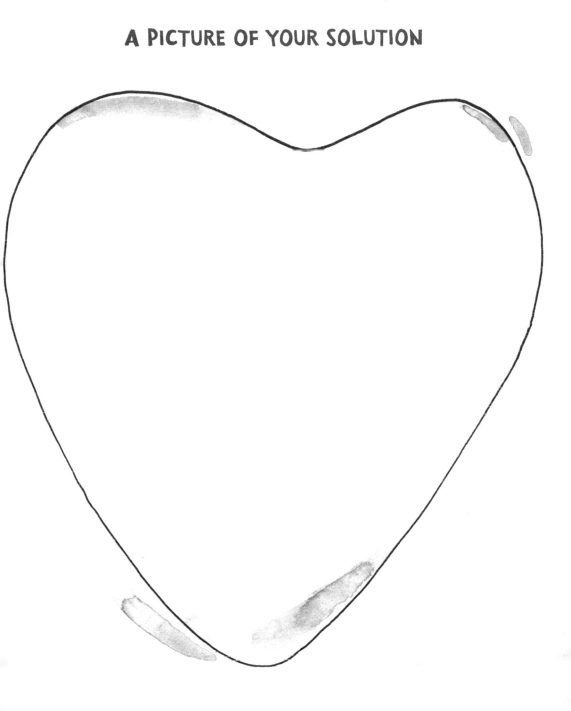

PROBLEM

No school is perfect. What would you do to improve yours?

SOLUTION

(by Robert, age 8)

"I would put chocolate milk in the water fountains."

What would you do to improve your school?

(by Lee Ann, age 8)

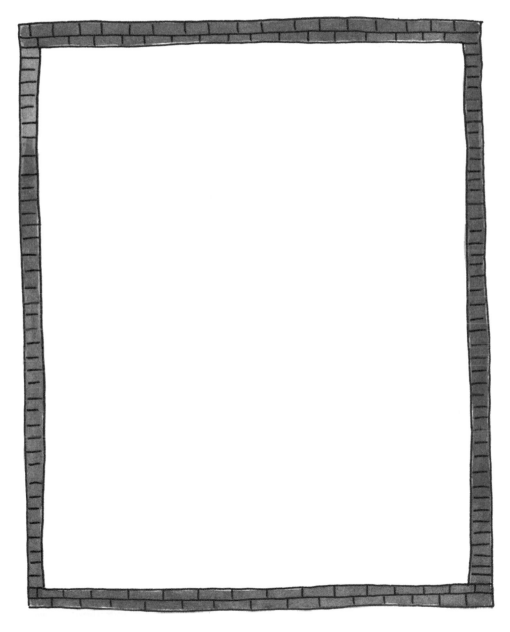

PROBLEM

Things are not always equal for boys and girls.
What can we do to fix that?

SOLUTION

(by Carla, age 8)

"Boys should be able to play house or Barbie. Why can't your dad do your hair? I think for one day girls should be boys and boys can be girls."

YOUR SOLUTION

How would you make things more equal?

Girl's solution (pretend you're a girl if you're not):

_____

_____

_____

_____

Boy's solution (pretend you're a boy if you're not):

_____

_____

_____

_____

A PICTURE OF YOUR FAVORITE SOLUTION

PROBLEM

Sometimes kids do things they know they shouldn't. Can you think of a way to keep kids out of trouble?

SOLUTION

(by Barrett, age 9)

"Open a carnival in every town."

YOUR SOLUTION

Why do you think kids get in trouble?

_____

_____

_____

Can you think of a good way to keep kids
out of trouble?

_____

_____

_____

A PICTURE OF YOUR SOLUTION

PROBLEM

What would you do for all the people who don't have homes?

SOLUTION

(by Helena, age 7)

"When people go away, like to their grandparents' house, the homeless people who live near them should live in their houses."

Don't forget to feed the fish!

YOUR SOLUTION

What would you do to help all the people who don't have homes?

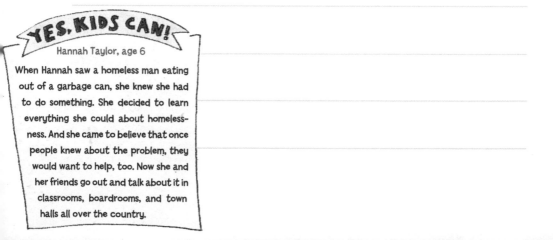

YES, KIDS CAN!

Hannah Taylor, age 6

When Hannah saw a homeless man eating out of a garbage can, she knew she had to do something. She decided to learn everything she could about homelessness. And she came to believe that once people knew about the problem, they would want to help, too. Now she and her friends go out and talk about it in classrooms, boardrooms, and town halls all over the country.

A PICTURE OF YOUR SOLUTION

What would you do to help the animals who don't have a place to live?

YES, KIDS CAN!

Janine Licare Andrews
and Aislin Livingstone, age 9

Janine and Aislin were worried about the animals who lose their homes when rain forests are cut down. They got their friends together and started raising money to save the trees. The money is also used to build bridges that keep the animals safe from cars and electrical wires.

SOLUTION
(by Craig, age 7)

"I would build a big place where
dogs can live and eat food."

What would you do for homeless animals?

A PICTURE OF YOUR SOLUTION

PROBLEM

There is a hole in the ozone, the layer of gas that protects Earth. What can we do to repair it?

SOLUTION
(by Sara, age 8)

"Get some dirt and seeds and plant flowers over the hole to make it look pretty for the aliens!"

YOUR SOLUTION

What would you do to help repair the hole in
the ozone?

_____

_____

_____

_____

_____

_____

A PICTURE OF YOUR SOLUTION

PROBLEM

Sometimes it seems like there is only bad news.

Can you come up with some good news?

SOLUTION

(by Caitlin, age 8)

"I got a new bike. And I'm having macaroni tonight."

What is your good news?

A PICTURE OF YOUR SOLUTION

PROBLEM

Help! Humans make so much garbage, we're running out of places to put it. What can we do?

SOLUTION
(by Kristin, age 10)

"Have a law that says every person who litters has to pick it up and eat it."

YOUR SOLUTION

What should we do about all the garbage?

A PICTURE OF YOUR SOLUTION

PROBLEM

Some people don't have jobs. A lot of people have jobs they don't like. Give their bosses some suggestions.

SOLUTION
(by Glenda, age 8)

"Let people have hamsters on their desks."

YOUR SOLUTION

 Find three people who have a job. Ask them what they don't like about their jobs.

1. _____

2. _____

3. _____

Come up with one suggestion for their bosses.

_____

_____

_____

_____

A PICTURE OF YOUR SOLUTION

PROBLEM

The economy has good times and bad times.
What do you recommend for the bad times?

SOLUTION

(by Jennifer, age 9)

"The government should have a bake sale."

YOUR SOLUTION

What do you recommend for a bad economy?

A PICTURE OF YOUR SOLUTION

PROBLEM

It seems like people who have lots of things want even more things, which leaves even fewer things for the people who did not have much to begin with. What can we do about this?

YES, KIDS CAN!

Evan Arnold, age 9

When Evan found out that some kids do not have what they need to play his favorite sport—baseball—he began collecting bats, mitts, balls, shoes, and money. Now he sends baseball gear to towns all over the world.

SOLUTION

(by Matthew, age 9)

"Everybody should have to give
up one thing."

YOUR SOLUTION

What would you do to get more people to share?

_____

_____

_____

_____

_____

_____

A PICTURE OF YOUR SOLUTION

Prejudice is when someone doesn't like you without knowing you, because of things like your skin color, religion, age, or size. Can you think of a cure for prejudice?

SOLUTION
(by Jonathan, age 10)

"If people act prejudiced, make them wear plaid jackets, plaid shirts, plaid pants, and plaid sneakers that say 'Don't be prejudiced' on them."

YOUR SOLUTION

Can you think of a cure for prejudice?

DON'T
BE
PREJUDICED
AGAINST
PLAID.

A PICTURE OF YOUR SOLUTION

PROBLEM

Nobody knows for sure why people start biting their nails, but almost everybody has some ideas about stopping. What are yours?

SOLUTION #1
(by Kelly, age 8)

"Stick your fingers in dog doo."

SOLUTION #2
(by Mitchell, age 8)

"Wear your shoes
on your hands."

SOLUTION #3
(by Caitlin, age 9)

"Put tinfoil on
your teeth."

YOUR SOLUTION

How would you get a nail-biter to stop?

A
what-
biter?

A PICTURE OF YOUR SOLUTION

PROBLEM

Some people are always shy and everyone is shy sometimes. How can you help a shy person feel less shy?

SOLUTION #1
(by Tiffany, age 7)

"Hold their hand."

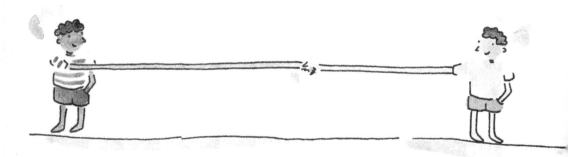

SOLUTION #2
(by Elisa, age 8)

"Ask them to sit with you."

SOLUTION #3
(by Christine, age 8)

"Sometimes you're not shy, you're just quiet."

YOUR SOLUTION

Are you ever shy? When and why?

How would you help a shy person feel less shy?

PROBLEM

Sometimes people feel bad about themselves. How can we help them feel better?

SOLUTION

(by Jacqueline, age 8)

"Everyone should have an alarm clock that says nice things to them in the morning when they wake up."

SNOOZE 1

I think you grew again! Let me see how tall and handsome you are...

SNOOZE 2

Your breath smells like flowers! You could almost skip brushing your teeth

SNOOZE 3

3 x 10 is 30 minutes, but I don't need to tell you - Mr. Math-whiz! Time to rise and shine, shine, shine!

SNOOZE 4

Good thing you're such a fast runner — here comes the bus!

How can we help people feel better about themselves?

_____

_____

_____

_____

_____

_____

_____

PROBLEM

When people are sick, they need extra-special care. How would you take care of someone who is sick?

SOLUTION

(by Noelle, age 8)

"I would let them have their pet in bed with them. And I would make medicine that tastes good."

THIS REALLY WORKS!

A lot of scientists say that having a pet or a friendly animal around helps you get better faster. Some hospitals allow pets to visit their patients. Others have their own animals, mainly cats and dogs, but sometimes even rabbits, small horses, goats, or pot-bellied pigs!

YOUR SOLUTION

What would make people feel better when they're sick?

 :

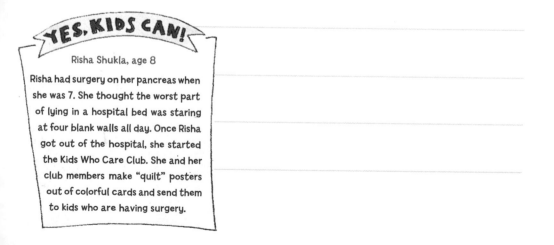

A PICTURE OF YOUR SOLUTION

PROBLEM

Everybody runs into bad luck sometimes. What do you do for good luck?

SOLUTION #1
(by Trista, age 7)

"I touch my brother's iguana."

LARRY

Touch 25¢ each
Kiss 50¢ each
Please pay first

SOLUTION #2
(by Ariele, age 7)

"Concentrate, practice, believe in yourself."

What do you do for good luck?

FIND ONE and KEEP IT HERE.

lucky penny

lucky eyelash

four-leaf clover

A PICTURE OF YOUR SOLUTION

PASTE A GOOD LUCK
COOKIE FORTUNE HERE

Most people (kids and grown-ups) need to exercise more. What can we do about that?

HOW MUCH is ENOUGH?

If you are a...	minutes every day
CAT	20
DOG	60
KID	60
GROWN UP	20
POTATO	0

SOLUTION
(by Patrick, age 8)

"Use special exercise shoes. When you get tired and want to go to sleep, too bad! These shoes will make you run until your feet fall off."

How can people get more exercise?

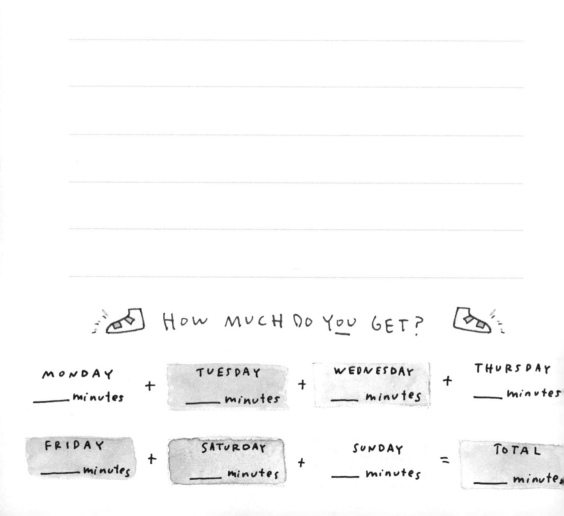

HOW MUCH DO YOU GET?

MONDAY
____ minutes

+

TUESDAY
____ minutes

+

WEDNESDAY
____ minutes

+

THURSDAY
____ minutes

FRIDAY
____ minutes

+

SATURDAY
____ minutes

+

SUNDAY
____ minutes

=

TOTAL
____ minutes

A PICTURE OF YOUR SOLUTION

PROBLEM

A lot of people have a hard time falling asleep. What would help?

Found a peanut...

SOLUTION #1
(by Elizabeth, age 8)

"Singing a song to them until they fall asleep."

THIS REALLY WORKS!
When you sing to babies, they listen. Bouncy play songs make babies more active. Lullabies (even when they are sung off-key) help babies focus their energy inward, calming and relaxing them so they can sleep.

SOLUTION #2

(by Joseph, age 8)

"Piling things up all around them so they feel safe."

How would you help someone fall asleep?

A PICTURE OF YOUR SOLUTION

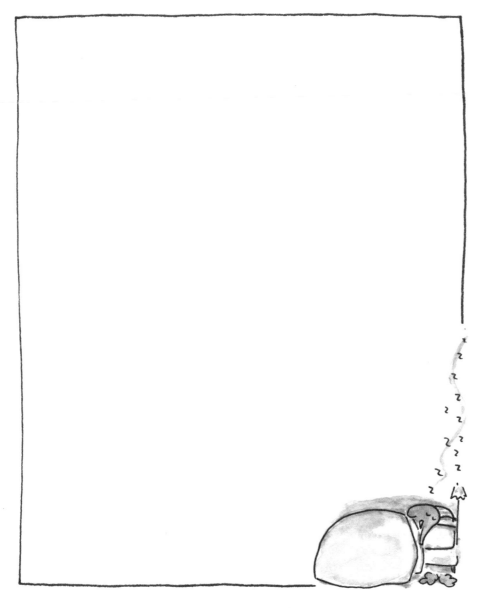

The biggest challenge is to get people up off their couches so they can go out and make the world better. Any ideas?

SOLUTION #1
(by Micah, age 10)

"Put spikes on all the couches."

SOLUTION #2

(by Julia, age 10)

"Start doing something yourself, or get someone who a lot of people like to start something."

How can we get people to do something about all or some or one of our world's problems?

_____

_____

_____

_____

_____

_____

_____

Once you're in the habit of thinking about problems, you may start to notice more of them—in your house, on the street, or in places you've never even heard of.

Noticing a problem is the first step toward finding a solution. Use these pages to work on problems wherever and whenever you notice them.

Today's date: _____

Problem: _____

Kind of problem:

- ☐ My own/personal
- ☐ My home/family
- ☐ My school/team/club
- ☐ My neighborhood/community
- ☐ My country/world

Possible solutions: _____

_____

_____

_____

Today's date: _____

Problem: _____

_____

Kind of problem:

☐ My own/personal

☐ My home/family

☐ My school/team/club

☐ My neighborhood/community

☐ My country/world

Possible solutions: _____

_____

_____

_____

Today's date: _____

Problem: _____

_____

Kind of problem:

☐ My own/personal

☐ My home/family

☐ My school/team/club

☐ My neighborhood/community

☐ My country/world

Possible solutions: _____

_____

_____

_____

Today's date: _____

Problem: _____

_____

Kind of problem:

☐ My own/personal

☐ My home/family

☐ My school/team/club

☐ My neighborhood/community

☐ My country/world

Possible solutions: _____

_____

_____

Today's date: _____

Problem: _____
_____

Kind of problem:

☐ My own/personal

☐ My home/family

☐ My school/team/club

☐ My neighborhood/community

☐ My country/world

Possible solutions: _____

_____

_____

_____

THE MAKE IT BETTER ACTION PLAN

You have thought about a lot of different problems. Now it's time to make an Action Plan and do something about one of them.

Step 1. Pick your problem. It can be the world's most important problem. Or it can be the problem that matters the most in the world to you. You can't go wrong—every problem can use your help!

PROBLEM:

_____

_____

_____

WHY THIS PROBLEM MATTERS TO ME:

_____

_____

_____

Step 2. The next step is to brainstorm to try to understand the problem. Ask yourself some questions, like:

WHY IS THIS PROBLEM A PROBLEM? WHAT CAUSES IT?

How wonderful it is
that nobody need wait
a single moment before starting
to improve the world.
— Anne Frank, age 12

Step 3. This problem could use your skills and talents. What are you good at?

MAKE AN OUTLINE OF YOUR HAND IN THE SPACE BELOW. WRITE ONE THING YOU ARE GOOD AT ON EACH FINGER.

Step 4. Now write down some ways to help fix the problem—maybe by using some of your skills.

WAYS TO FIX THIS PROBLEM:

You can change the world with your own two hands.

Step 5. Pick one of your ideas. Which solution do you want to try first?

MY SOLUTION: _____

_____

_____

Step 6. Share your solution. Show two people you know—a friend, a parent, a teacher, or anyone who can help you fix the problem—and see what they think.

HELPER'S NAME: _____

HELPER'S IDEAS: _____

_____

HELPER'S NAME: _____

HELPER'S IDEAS: _____

_____

Find out if there are groups already at work on your problem. Write a letter or e-mail to tell the group about your solution. Ask if there are other things you could do to help.

GROUP'S NAME:

GROUP'S IDEAS:

Step 7. Using the new ideas you gathered, rethink your solution and write it here. Your new and improved solution is your Mission.

MY MISSION:

Step 8. Get moving. Make a list of what you need to do in order to accomplish your Mission. Then go out and do it!

SOME POSSIBLE TO-DOS:

- Make phone calls
- Find helpers
- Give helpers jobs
- Raise money
- Get supplies
- Make posters
- Write thank-you notes

SOME POSSIBLE HELPERS:

- Family
- Friends
- Teachers
- Librarians
- School groups
- Community groups
- Businesses
- Government officials

MY TO-DO LIST

TO DO:	DONE
1. Write mission	☑
2.	☐
3.	☐
4. Remember why it's important	☐
5.	☐
6.	☐
7.	☐
8.	☐
9.	☐
10. Celebrate!	☐

GET CONNECTED!

Find help, more ideas, and other kids who want to change the world through the following websites.

www.4-h.org Millions of kids, ages 5 to 19, pledge to make a difference in their communities through their work in 4-H clubs. Join a club in your area.

www.compassionatekids.com Compassionate Kids is for grown-ups who want to help kids learn kindness toward the earth, people, and animals. The website features kid-friendly community service events and field trips.

www.oxfam.org.uk/coolplanet/kidsweb Oxfam was started in England to work on hunger. At Cool Planet, you can learn about hunger around the world and then help put an end to it. (You can also learn how to recycle a cell phone and get your school involved.)

www.girlscouts.org (Girl Scouts), **www.scouting.org** (Boy Scouts) You can learn skills that will help you make the world a better place. And you and your troop will get to do lots of fun stuff, including community service projects.

www.globalresponse.org/kidsactions.php Global Response has information and ideas for kids who want to work on the environment.

www.idealist.org/kt Get ideas, inspiration, and information to start your own project or volunteer for somebody else's.

www.kidscare.org Kids Care Club members have fun serving their communities. You can try out their ideas, become a member, or start a club in your hometown.

www.kidssavetherainforest.org Find out more about Janine and Aislin and their work to save the rain forest and the animals in the Manuel Antonio area of Costa Rica.

www.kidswhocareclub.org Help Risha Shukla with her mission by joining the Kids Who Care Club or come up with your own project to cheer up kids who are sick.

www.kindnews.org If you want to help animals, Kind News is a good place to start. You can find out about animal causes and get ideas from the experts at The Humane Society.

www.ladybugfoundation.ca Hannah Taylor and her friends started The Ladybug Foundation to help end homelessness. Find out more about homelessness and Hannah's work on their website.

www.pbskids.org/zoom/activities/action Zoom into Action has lots of volunteer opportunities. You can send in a story about your project or get inspired by somebody else's.

www.randomkid.org You can start or grow your own project with Random Kid or you can plug into another kid's project and help it grow.

www.rootsandshoots.org/kidsandteens There are Roots and Shoots kids all over the world working on improving care for the environment, animal, and human communities. You can join a Roots and Shoots Club near you (or get your school to start one), or you can be part of an online campaign.

www.ryanswell.ca Ryan Hreljac's foundation works on his dream that everyone should have clean drinking water. Learn about the problems with water and help Ryan make his dream come true.

www.timeforkids.com Learn more about your cause at *Time* magazine's kid-friendly site.

http://youth.foundationcenter.org At Youth in Philanthropy, you can read about other kids' projects and find out more ways to get involved in your own community.

www.ysa.org Youth Service America's website has information and opportunities for kids ages 5 to 25 (and their parents).

CONGRATULATIONS! You did it. You helped make the world a better place. Thank you!

WHAT WAS THE BEST PART OF YOUR ACTION PLAN? WHAT WAS THE WORST PART?

WHAT WOULD YOU DO DIFFERENTLY NEXT TIME?

WHAT'S NEXT?

CERTIFICATE OF HONOR

This certificate is hereby awarded to

_____

on _____

in recognition of exceptional service to the community
and an ongoing commitment to making a better world.